The Night Before Christmas
at 221-B

Joseph W. Svec III
&
Lidia Svec

The Night Before Christmas
at 221-B

By
Joseph W. Svec III
&
Lidia Svec

Paperback ISBN 9781787056756

Published in the UK by MX Publishing
335 Princess Park Manor, Royal Drive, London, N11 3GX
www.mxpublishing.com

Cover compiled by Brian Belanger

Illustrations by Clipart.com

The authors may be contacted via their web page,
www.pixymuse.com or their Facebook page
www.facebook.com/sherlockgrinningcat

Acknowledgements

We would like to thank our son Joe, for appearing as Dr. Watson, and his wife Priscilla, for portraying Mrs.Hudson.

We would like to thank Rysia our German Shepherd, for playing the part of "a hound".

We would like to thank Clement Clarke Moore for the original poem, on which this is based.

We would like to offer a special thanks to Linda Hein of Baker Street West for use of the museum quality recreation of Sherlock Holmes' lodgings, 221-B as the location of our photos. Baker Street West, of 204 Main Street, in Jackson California, is a non-profit organization, dedicated to fostering interest in Victorian culture and the works of Sir Arthur Conan Doyle, and others of the period, by producing events, and a venue for these activities to take place.

Besides being the location of the West Coast's finest recreation of 221-B Baker Street, and a haven for all things Sherlockian, Baker Street West is also the location of Victorian Square, a collection of eight unique shoppes, straight from the world of Sherlock Holmes. The shoppes include; Mrs. Hudson's Tea Shoppe, Dr. Watson's Apothecary, Irene Adler's Emporium, The Deerstalker, South Down's Apiary, Wiggin's Toy Shoppe, Stewart's Scientifics, and the Wolf and Bear Pub.

More information can be found at www.Bakerstreetwest.com

Introduction

The poem, *A Visit from Saint Nicholas*, more commonly known as *The Night Before Christmas*, was first published anonymously in 1823, and later attributed to Clement Clarke Moore. It tells the story of a gentleman who is visited by Saint Nicholas on Christmas Eve, and it has become a holiday favorite over the years. It has spawned many offspring, including specialized variations, dealing with parents trying to assemble Christmas toys, computer age versions and several different regional settings.

In reading the original, I wondered, what if I were to tell the story from the viewpoint of Sherlock Holmes and Dr. Watson? And so, it is, you have the story-poem in your hands, *The Night Before Christmas at 221-B*

The Night Before Christmas
at 221-B

T'was the night before Christmas at 221-B
But presents were missing from under the tree.

In deep contemplation, Sherlock with care,
Stood pondering, wondering, why weren't they there?

Mrs. Hudson was nestled all snug in her bed,
While visions of Earl Grey danced in her head.

Holmes in his robe, and his deer stalker cap,
Had just woken up from a short winter's nap.

For out on the lawn there arose such a clatter,
He had sprung from his chair to see what was the matter.

On his way to the window, he had noticed the tree. There were no presents. Now how could that be?

ELEMENTARY,
MY DEAR
WATSON

The light of the moon on that cold winter's night
Gave an eerie glow to the presentless sight.

When what to his wondering eyes did appear,
But a clue on the floor, he saw it quite clear.

He analyzed, and scrutinized, his skills so very quick.
He knew in a moment it was all a subtle trick.

More rapid than eagles, his answers they came.
His deductions were many, he called them by name;

"Illusions and mirrors, and curtains, and more,
Look at that odd bit of cord on the floor!

Enough of this riddle, enough of these schemes,
I know what is here is not what it seems.

He turned up the light, and as easy as pie,
Pulled back the curtain and, then gave a sigh,

for just as he thought, just as he knew,
There were the presents, and John Watson, too.

And then in a twinkling, like rain on the roof,
The good Doctor said, "I now have my proof.

More than anything else, not even a hound,
You love a good mystery, when one can be found.

You really must say, old boy, plainly put,
You're at your best when the game is afoot.

I set this all up, I do have the knack,
A riddle, a mystery for you to crack."

Sherlock's eyes how they twinkled, for he was so merry.
How quickly he had solved this yuletide query.

Sherlock then held two glasses, as clear as the snow,
"Let us now toast with this fine Bordeaux.

You have done it old friend; you've made my day!
The best present ever, I really must say."

But then they both heard, as the night turned to dawn,
A ruckus, a rumpus, outside on the lawn.

They turned to the widow, and looked out right quick,
And who did they see, but jolly Saint Nick,

In his sleigh drawn by reindeer, he paused just a while,
He looked up to them, winked, and said with a smile,

"I left you your gifts, they are under the tree,
A spyglass for Sherlock, for Watson, some tea.

And for your landlady, the best, I've heard say,
A chest of the finest of teas, Earl Grey.

Then they heard him exclaim, ere he drove out of sight—
"Happy Christmas to all, and to all a good night!"

Also from MX Publishing

MX Publishing is the largest Sherlock Holmes publisher in the world with over 500 books and more than two hundred authors.

We have several Christmas books, including one of the 24 Volumes of the MX Book of New Sherlock Holmes Stories (Volume V) with dozens of Christmas themed tales and several advent calendars too.

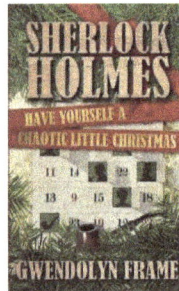

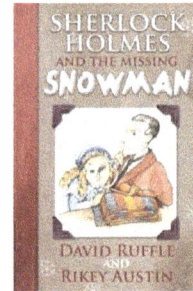

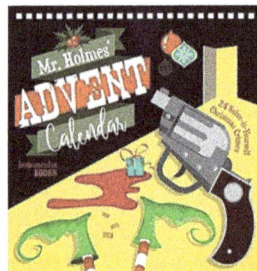

You can find out all about MX and our social enterprise at mxpublishing.com, on Twitter and Instagram @mxpublishing and on facebook.com/mxpublishing

liance